D0804436

MY BROTHER IN THE WHITE HOUSE

Corinne Roosevelt Robinson

first published as Chapters 9-10 of

MY BROTHER THEODORE ROOSEVELT

PREFACE

This Preface I write to my fellow countrymen as I give into their hands these intimate reminiscences of my brother, Theodore Roosevelt.

A year and a half ago I was invited by the City History Club of New York to make an address about my brother on Washington's Birthday. Upon being asked what I would call my speech, I replied that as George Washington was the "Father of his country," as Abraham Lincoln was the "Saviour of his country," so Theodore Roosevelt was the "Brother of his country," and that, therefore, the subject of my speech would be "The Brother of His Country."

In the same way, I feel that in giving to the public these almost confidential personal recollections, I do so because of the attitude of that very public toward Theodore Roosevelt. There is no sacrilege in sharing such memories with the people who have loved him, and whom he loved so well.

This book is not a biography, it is not a political history of the times, although I have been most careful in the effort to record facts accurately, and carefully to search my memory before relating conversations or experiences; it is, I hope, a clear picture, drawn at close hand by one who, because of her relationship to him and her intercourse with him, knew his loyalty and tenderness of heart in a rare and satisfying way, and had unusual opportunity of comprehending the point of view, and therefore perhaps of clarifying the point of view, of one of the great Americans of the day.

As I have reread his letters to me, as I have dwelt upon our long and devoted friendship—for we were even more friends than brother and sister—his character stands out to me more stronglyviii than ever before as that of "The Great Sharer." He shared all that he had—his worldly goods, his strong mentality, his wide sympathy, his joyous fun, and his tender comprehension—with all those with whom he came in contact, and especially with those closest and dearest to him—the members of his own family and his sisters.

In the spirit of confidence that my frankness will not be misunderstood, I place a sister's interpretation of a world-wide personality in the hands of my fellow Americans.

Corinne Roosevelt
Robinson
September, 1921.

With tender affection
I dedicate this book
to my sister
ANNA ROOSEVELT
COWLES
whose unselfish
devotion to her
brother
THEODORE
ROOSEVELT
never wavered
through his whole
life, and for whom he
had from childhood a
deep and unswerving
love and admiration

Uncrowned the brow,
Where truth and
courage meet,
The citizen alone
confronts the land.

* * * * *

A man whose
dreamful, valiant
mind conceives
High purpose,
consecrated to his
race.

—Margaret Ridgely
Partridge.

PART ONE

The deed of the cowardly assassin had done its work. William McKinley was dead; the young Vice-President had made the hazardous trip from the heart of the Adirondack Mountains, had taken the solemn oath in Buffalo, had followed the body of his chief to the final resting-place, and had returned to Washington. From Washington he telegraphed to my husband and myself, with the thought which he always showed, and told us that as Mrs. Roosevelt was attending to last important matters at Sagamore, she could not be with him the day he moved into the White House, and that he was very anxious that not only my sister, Mrs. Cowles, and her husband, but that we also should dine with him the first night that he slept in the old mansion. So we went on to Washington, and were with him at that first meal in the house for which he had such romantic attachment because it had sheltered the hero of his boyhood and manhood, Abraham Lincoln. As we sat around the table he turned and said: "Do you realize that this is the birthday of our father, September 22? I have realized it as I signed various papers all day long, and I feel that it is a good omen that I begin my duties in this house on this day. I feel as if my father's hand were on my shoulder, and as if there were a special blessing over the life I am to lead here." Almost as he finished this sentence, the coffee was passed to us, and at that time it was the habit at the White House to pass with the coffee a little boutonnière to each gentleman.

As the flowers were passed to the President, the one given to him was a yellow saffronia rose. His face flushed, and he turned again and said: "Is it not strange! This is the rose we all connect with my father." My sister and I responded eagerly that many a time in the past we had seen our father pruning the rose-bush of saffronia roses with special care. He always picked one for his buttonhole from that bush, and whenever we gave him a rose, we gave him one of those. Again my brother said, with a very serious look on his face, "I think there is a blessing connected with this," and surely it did seem as if there were a blessing connected with those years of Theodore Roosevelt in the White House; those merry happy years of family life, those ardent, loving years of public service, those splendid, peaceful years of international amity—a blessing there surely was over that house.

Nothing could have been harder to the temperament of Theodore Roosevelt than to have come "through the cemetery," as Peter Dunne said in his prophetic article, to the high position of President of the United States. What he had achieved in the past was absolutely through his own merits. To him to come to any position through "dead men's shoes" was peculiarly distasteful; but during the early years of his occupancy of the White House, feeling it his duty so to do, he strove in every possible way to fulfil the policies of his predecessor, retaining his appointees and working with conscientious loyalty as much as possible along the lines laid down by President McKinley.

That first winter of his incumbency was one of special interest. Many were the difficulties in his path. England, and, indeed, all foreign countries were watching him with deep interest. I realized that fact in a very special way as that very spring of 1902 I took my young daughter abroad to place her at a French school directed by Mademoiselle Souvestre in England. It was the spring when preparations were being made for the coronation of

King Edward VII, and because of the fact that I was the sister of the President of the United States, I was received with great courtesy. Our dear friend Mr. Joseph H. Choate was then ambassador to England. Mrs. Choate presented me at court, and the King paid me the unusual compliment—out of respect to my brother—of leaving the dais on which he and the Queen stood, and came forward to greet me personally in order to ask for news of my brother. Special consideration was shown to me in so many ways that when Mr. Robinson and I were visiting Edinburgh, it seemed in no way unusual that we should be invited to

Holyrood Castle to the reception given by the lord high commissioner, Lord Leven and Melville. It so happened that we were in Edinburgh during that week of festivity when the lord high commissioner of Scotland, appointed as special representative of the King of Great Britain, holds court in the old castle as though he were actually the King.

We had dined with friends before the reception, and were therefore late in reaching the castle, and were literally the last people at the end of the long queue approaching the dais on which Lord and Lady Leven and Melville stood.

As King Edward had himself stepped forward to meet me in Buckingham Palace, I was not surprised when Lord Leven and Melville stepped down from the dais, and I expected him also to ask news of my brother, the President of the United States, as King Edward had done, but to my great surprise, and be it confessed

intense pleasure,
I heard the lord
high commissioner
speak as follows:
"Mrs. Douglas
Robinson, you have
been greeted with
special courtesy
in our country
because of your
distinguished brother,
the President of the
United States, but
I am greeting you
with even greater
interest because of

your father, the first Theodore Roosevelt. You probably do not remember, for you were a little girl at the time, that a raw-boned young Scotchman named Ronald Leslie Melville came long ago to New York and was much at your home, having had letters of introduction to your father as one of the men best fitted to teach him the modern philanthropic methods used in America. Only to-day," he continued, "I told the children of Edinburgh, assembled, as is the custom, to listen to the lord high commissioner, that the father of the present President of the United States was the first man who taught me to love my fellow men."

My heart was very
full as I made
my courtesy and
answered the lord
high commissioner.
Before he let me pass
on he said, with a
charming smile: "If
you and Mr. Robinson
will come tomorrow
to lunch with us
quietly I will take
you to Lord Darnley's
room, which is my

dressing-room during the week of Holyrood festivities, and on my dressing-table you will see the photograph of your father, for I never go anywhere without it." I accepted the invitation gladly, and the next day we went to Holyrood Castle, lunched informally with the delightful chatelain and chatelaine, and

I was taken, as the former promised, to see Lord Damley's room, where my father's face smiled at me from the dressing-table. My brother loved to hear me tell this story, and I feel that it is not amiss to include it in any recollections concerning my brother, for he was truly the spirit of my father reincarnate.

In May, 1902, Mrs. Roosevelt writes that "Theodore" is just about to leave for a hunting trip, which she hopes will "rest" him. (The rest the year before, of writing a life of Oliver Cromwell, had not been made quite strenuous enough for a real rest!) Later he returned and made a famous speech in Providence, a speech epoch-making, and recognized as such by an English newspaper, The Morning Post of August 27, 1902, a clipping from which I have at hand, and which runs as follows:

"Our New York correspondent announced yesterday that President Roosevelt's great speech at Providence on the subject of

'Trusts' is regarded
on all sides and
by both parties
as an absolutely
epoch-making
event. This is not
surprising to those
who have studied
the conditions of
American politics,
and the merits of the
particular economic
question involved,
so far as they are
intelligible to us, or
last but by no means

least, the character and personality of President Roosevelt. It would now seem that the people of the United States are at the parting of the ways between the corrupt, old political system and a newer, manlier, honester conception of public rights and duties."

Perhaps this sentence foreshadows more

than any other contemporary expression the enormous instrument for honesty in high places in the history of his country which it was Theodore Roosevelt's destiny to be.

Mingled with these great cares and far-reaching issues came, later, brighter moments, and it was

about that time that
during an interval
of play at Oyster
Bay, he started the
custom of his famous
"obstacle walks."
He would gather all
the little cousins
and his own children
and mine, if I could
bring them down
for a week-end, on
Sunday afternoon
at Sagamore Hill
(even an occasional
"grown person"

was considered
sufficiently
adventurous to
be included in the
party), and would
start on one of the
strenuous scrambles
which he called an
"obstacle walk."
It was more like a
game than a walk,
for it had rules and
regulations of its
own, the principal
one being that
each participant

should follow the presidential leader "over or through" any obstacle but never "around." There were sometimes as many as twenty little children as we stood on the top of Cooper's Bluff, a high sand-bank overlooking the Sound, ready for the word "go," and all of them children were agog with excitement at the probable obstacles in their path. As we stood on the brink of the big sand-bank, my brother would turn with an amused twinkle in his eye and say: "There is a little path down the side, but I always jump off the top." This, needless to say, was in the form of a challenge, which he always accompanied by a laugh and a leap into the air, landing on whatever portion of his body happened to be the one that struck the lower part of the sand-bank first. Then there would be a shout from the children, and every one would imitate his method of progress, I myself, generally the only other grown person, bringing up the rear rather reluctantly but determined not to have to follow the other important rule of the game, which was that if you could not succeed in going "over or through" that you should put your metaphorical tail between your physical legs and return home. You were not jeered at, no disagreeable remark was directed at you, but your sense of failure was humiliation enough.

Having reached the foot of the bank in this promiscuous fashion, we would all sit on stones and take off our shoes and stockings to shake the quantities of sand therefrom, and then start on the real business of the day. With a sense of great excitement we watched our leader and the devious course he pursued while finding the most trying obstacles to test our courage. I remember one day seeing in our path an especially unpleasant-looking little bathing-house with a very steep roof like a Swiss chalet. I looked at it with sudden dismay, for I realized that only the very young and slender could chin up its slippery sides, and I hoped that the leader of the party would deflect his course. Needless to say, he did not, and I can still see the somewhat sturdy body of the then President of the United States hurling itself at the obstruction and

with singular agility
chinning himself to
the top and sliding
down on the other
side. The children
stormed it with
whoops of delight,
but I thought I
had come to my
Waterloo. Just as I
had decided that the
moment had come
for that ignominious
retreat of which I
have already spoken,
I happened to notice

a large rusty nail on one side of the unfinished shanty, and I thought to myself: "If I can get a footing on that nail, then perhaps I can get my hands to the top of that sloping roof, and if I can get my hands there, perhaps by Herculean efforts I too can chin myself over the other side." Nothing succeeds like success, for having performed this almost impossible feat and having violently returned into the midst of my anxious group of fellow pedestrians, very much as the little boy does on his sled on the steepest snow-clad hill, I was greeted with an ovation such as I have never received in later life for the most difficult achievement, literary or philanthropic! From that moment I was regarded as one really fit to take part in the beloved "obstacle walks," which were, I cannot help but think, strong factors in planting in the hearts and characters of the children who thus followed their leader, the indomitable pluck and determination which helped the gallant sons and nephews of Theodore Roosevelt to go undauntedly "over the top" on Flanders Field.

"Over or through, never around"—a good motto, indeed, for Young America, and one which was always exemplified by that American of Americans, my brother, Theodore Roosevelt.

At the end of October that year, his affectionate concern for me (for I was delicate at the time) takes form in a lovely letter in which, after giving me the best of advice, and acknowledging humorously that no one ever really took advice offered, he says: "Heaven bless you always whether you take my advice or not." He never failed to show loving and tender interest in the smallest of my pleasures or anxieties, nor did he and Mrs. Roosevelt ever fail to invite, at my instigation, elderly family friends to lunch at the White House, or gladly to send me autographs for many little boys, or checks to "Dolly," the nurse of his childhood, whose advanced years I superintended.

In April, 1903, he started on a long trip, and at that time felt that, as the years of his inherited incumbency were drawing to a close, he could forward his own gospel. A humorous reference comes in a letter just before he starts, in which he says: "I was immensely amused with Monroe's message [my second son, then at St. Paul's School] about boxing and confirmation, the one evidently having some occult connection with the other in his mind.

Give him my love when you write.... Well, I start on a nine-weeks' trip tomorrow, as hard a trip as I have ever undertaken, with the sole exception of the canvass in 1900. As a whole, it will be a terrific strain, but there will be an occasional day which I shall enjoy."

Again, as he actually

starts on that "hard" trip, he sends me a little line of never-failing love. "White House, April 1, 1903. [This in his own writing.] Darling Pussie: Just a last line of Good-bye. I am so glad your poor hand is better at last. Love to dear old Douglas. The house seems strange and lonely without the children. Ever yours, T. R." Those little notes in his own dear handwriting, showing always the loving thought, are especially precious and treasured.

After that exhausting journey, replete with many thrilling experiences, he returns to Oyster Bay for a little rest, and writes with equal interest of the beautiful family life which was always led there. My boy Stewart was with him at the time, and he speaks of him affectionately in connection with his own "Ted," who was Stewart's intimate friend:

"Stewart, Ted and I took an hour and a half bareback ride all together. Ted is always longing that Stewart should go off on a hunting trip with him. I should be delighted to have them go off now. Although I think no doubt they would get into scrapes, I have also no doubt that they would get out of them. We have had a lovely summer, as lovely a summer as we have ever passed. All the children have enjoyed their various activities, and we have been a great deal with the children, and in addition to that, Edith and I have ridden on horseback much together, and have frequently gone off for a day at a time in a little row boat, not to speak of the picnics to which everybody went.

"In the intervals
I have chopped
industriously. I have
seen a great many
people who came
to call upon me on
political business. I
have had to handle
my correspondence
of course, and I
have had not a few
wearing matters
of national policy,
ranging from the
difficulties in Turkey
to the scandals in

the Post Office. But I have had three months of rest, of holiday, by comparison with what has gone before. Next Monday I go back to Washington, and for the thirteen months following, there will be mighty little let-up to the strain. But I enjoy it to the full.

"What the outcome

will be as far as I am personally concerned, I do not know. It looks as if I would be renominated; whether I shall be re-elected I haven't the slightest idea. I know there is bitter opposition to me from many sources. Whether I shall have enough support to overcome this opposition, I cannot tell. I suppose few Presidents can form the slightest idea whether their policies have met with approval or not. Certainly I cannot. But as far as I can see, these policies have been right, and I hope that time will justify them. If it doesn't why I must abide the fall of the dice, and that is all there is to it. Ever yours, T. R."

That letter is very characteristic of his usual attitude. Strain, yes; hard work, yes; but equally "I enjoy it to the full"! Equally also was he willing to abide by the "fall of the dice," having done what he fully believed to have been the right thing for the country.

That December, the day after Christmas,

he writes again:

"Darling Sister: I so enjoyed seeing you here, but I have been so worried about you. I am now looking forward to Stewart's coming, and to seeing Helen and Ted. But I do wish you would take a rest.

"We had a delightful Christmas yesterday, just such a Christmas as thirty or forty years ago we used to have under Father's and Mother's supervision in 28 East 20th Street. At seven all the children came in to open the big, bulging stockings in our bed; Kermit's terrier, Allan, a most friendly little dog, adding to the children's delight by occupying the middle of the bed. From Alice to

Quentin, each child was absorbed in his or her stocking, and Edith certainly managed to get the most wonderful stocking toys.... Then after breakfast we all went into the library, where the bigger toys were on separate tables for the children. I wonder whether there ever can come in life a thrill of greater exaltation and rapture than that which comes to one, say between the ages of six and fourteen, when the library doors are thrown open and one walks in to see all the gifts, like a materialized fairyland, arrayed on one's own special table.

"We had a most pleasant lunch at

Bamie's [our sister, Mrs. Cowles]. She had given a delightful Christmas tree to the children the afternoon before, and then I stopped in to see Cabot and Nannie [Senator and Mrs. Lodge]. It was raining so hard that we could not walk or ride with any comfort, so Roly Fortescue, Ted and I played 'single stick' in the study later. All of our connections and all of the Lodge connections were at dinner with us, twenty-two in all. After the dinner we danced in the 'East Room,' closing with the Virginia Reel,— Edith looking as young and as pretty, and dancing as well as ever.

"It is a clear, cold

morning, and Edith and I and all the children (save Quentin) and also Bob Ferguson and Cabot are about to start for a ride. Your loving brother."

Such were all Christmases at the White House; such was the spirit of the White House in those days.

During the early

years of my brothers presidency, my husband and I always spent Thanksgiving at the White House, and joined in festivities very much like the Christmas ones, including the gay Virginia reel, which was also part, always, of the Thanksgiving ceremony. After they bought a little place in Virginia, they spent their Thanksgiving anniversary there.

During the following winter, I visited the White House more frequently than usual, and enjoyed the special ceremonies such as the diplomatic dinner, judicial reception, etc., and I used to station myself near the President when he was receiving the long line of eager fellow citizens, and watch his method of welcoming his guests. Almost always he would have some special word for each, and although the long line would not be held back, for he was so rapid in speech that the individual welcome would hardly take a moment, still almost every person who passed

him would have had
that extraordinary
sense that he or
she was personally
recognized. It was
either a reference
to the splendid old
veteran father of
one, or some devoted
sacrifice on the part
of the mother of
another, or a deed of
valor of the person
himself, or a merry
reminiscence of
hunting or Rough

Rider warfare;
but with each and
every person who
passed in what
seemed occasionally
an interminable
line, there was
immediately
established a
personal sense of
relationship. Perhaps
that was, of all my
brother's attributes,
the most endearing,
namely, that power
of his of injecting

himself into the life of the other person and of making that other person realize that he was not just an indifferent lump of humanity, but a living and breathing individual coming in contact with another individual even more vividly alive.

After my own visit of special festivity I apparently suggest certain people for him to ask to the White House, or at least I ask him to see them, for in a letter, also in his own handwriting, on February 21, 1904, he says: "Thank you for suggesting F. W. I am glad you told me; it was thoughtful of you. I will also try to see B——, but I don't know whether it will do any good.

He is a kind, upright, typical bourgeois of the purely mercantile type; and however much we respect each other, we live in widely different and sundered worlds." So characteristic, this last sentence. Willing he always was to try to do what I wished or thought wise, but also he was always frank in giving me the reason why he felt my wish, in some cases, would bear but little fruit. The bourgeois, mercantile type did indeed live in a different and sundered world from that of the practical idealist, Theodore Roosevelt.

In the summer of 1904, when again I was far from well, he writes from the White House, August

14: "Darling Corinne: The news in your letter greatly worried me. I wish I could call to see you and try to amuse you. I think of you always. Let me know at once, or have Douglas let me know, how you are. Edith came back here for a week with me, and we had a real honeymoon time together. Then she went back to the children.... Every spare moment has been occupied with preparing my letter of acceptance. No one can tell how the election will turn out; but I am more than content, whatever comes, for I have been able to do much that was worth doing. With love to Douglas and very, very much love to you, I am, Your devoted

Brother." In the midst of the pressing cares of the administration and the fatigue of his letter of acceptance he still has time for the usual unfailing interest in me and mine!

On October 18, again my brother writes:

"Of course, I am excited about the election, but there really isn't much

I can do about it, and I confine myself chiefly to the regular presidential work. Nobody can tell anything about the outcome. At the present time, it looks rather favorable to me." And again to my husband on October 25: "As for the result, the Lord only knows what it will be. Appearances look favorable, but I have a mind steeled for any outcome!"

In spite of his "mind steeled for any outcome," the one great ambition of Theodore Roosevelt's life was to be chosen President on his own merits by the people of the United States. He longed for the seal of approval on the devoted service which he had rendered to his country, and one of my clearest memories is my conversation with him on Election day, 1904, when on his way back from voting at Oyster Bay, I met him at Newark, N. J., and went with him as far as Philadelphia. In his private drawing-room on the car, he opened his heart to me, and told me that

he had never wanted
anything in his life
quite as much as the
outward and visible
sign of his country's
approval of what
he had done during
the last three and a
half years. I frankly
do not feel that this
wish was because
of any overweening
ambition on his part,
but to the nature of
Theodore Roosevelt
it had always been

especially difficult to have come into the great position which he held through a calamity to another rather than as the personal choice of the people of the United States. His temperament was such that he wished no favor which he had not himself won. Therefore, it seemed to him a crucial moment in his life when, on his own merit, he was to be judged as fit or unfit to be his own successor. Not only for those reasons did he wish to be elected in his own right, but because, as was the case in former days when he wished to be renominated governor of New York State, he had again initiated many reforms, and had made many appointments, and he wished to carry those reforms into effect and to back up those appointments with his own helpfulness and prestige.

When we parted in Philadelphia, I to return to my home in Orange and he to go on to meet this vital moment of his career, I remember feeling a poignant anxiety about the result of the election, and it can well be understood the joy I felt that evening when the returns proved him overwhelmingly successful at the polls. Late at night, we received a telegram from the White House directed to Mr. and Mrs. Douglas Robinson in answer to our wire sent earlier in the evening. It ran as follows: "Was glad to hear from you. Only wish you were with us this evening." The next morning I received a letter, only a few lines but infinitely characteristic. They were penned by my brother upon his arrival at the White House after we had parted in Philadelphia, some hours before he knew anything of the election returns. In this letter he describes his sudden reaction from the condition of nervous excitement from which he had suffered during the day. He says: "As I mounted the White House steps, Edith came to meet me at the door, and I suddenly realized that, after all, no matter what the outcome of the election should prove to be; my happiness was assured, even though my ambition to have the seal of approval put upon my administration might not be gratified,—for my life with Edith and my children constitutes my happiness." This little note posted to me on the eve of his great victory showed clearly his sense of proportion and his conception of true values.

On November 11, 1904, he writes again: "Darling Corinne: I received your letter. I have literally but one moment in which to respond, for I am swamped with letters and telegrams. We have received between eight and ten thousand. I look forward with keen eagerness to seeing you and Douglas."

And so the crucial moment was over, and by a greater majority than had ever before been known in this country, the man of destiny had come into his own, and Theodore Roosevelt, acclaimed by all the people whom he had served so faithfully, was, in his own right and through no sad misfortune, President of the United States of America.

Almost immediately after the excitement of the election, namely, on November

12, 1904, my brother writes to my husband: "If you and Corinne could come on with us to the St. Louis Fair, it would be the greatest possible delight. Now, for Heaven's sake, don't let anything interfere with both of your coming."

Needless to say, we accepted the invitation joyfully,

and the trip to the St. Louis Fair was one of our most unique experiences. Coming as it did almost immediately after the great victory of his overwhelming election, wherever the train stopped he received a tremendous ovation, and my memory of him during the transit is equally one of cheering groups and swarming delegations.

In spite of the noise and general excitement, whenever he had a spare moment of quiet, I noticed that he always returned to his own special seat in a corner of the car, and became at once completely absorbed in two large volumes which were always ready on his chair for him. The rest of us would read irrelevantly, perhaps, talk equally irrelevantly, and the hours sped past; but my brother, when he was not actually receiving delegations or making an occasional impromptu speech at the rear end of the car to the patient, waiting groups who longed to show him their devotion, would return in the most detached and focussed manner to the books in which he absorbed himself.

Our two days at St. Louis were the type of days only led by a presidential party at a fair. Before experiencing them I had thought it would be rather "grand" to be a President's sister, with the aforesaid President when he opened a great fair. "Grand"it certainly was, but the exhaustion outbalanced the grandeur. I ran steadily for forty-eight hours without one moment's intermission. My brother never seemed to walk at all, and my whole memory of the St. Louis Fair is a perpetual jog-trot, only interrupted by interminable receptions, presentations of gifts, lengthy luncheons and lengthier evening banquets, and I literally remember *no night* at all! Whether we never went to bed during the time we were at the fair, or exactly what happened to the nights after twelve o'clock, is more than I can say. At the end of the time allotted for the fair, after the last long banquet, we returned to our private car, and I can still see the way in which my sister-in-law (she was not *born* a Roosevelt!) fell into her stateroom. I was about to follow her example (it was midnight) when my brother turned to me in the gayest possible manner and said: "Not going to bed, are you!" "Well," I replied, "I *had thought* of it." "But no," he said; "I told my stenographer this morning to rest all day, for I knew that I would need her services to-night, and now she is perfectly rested." I interrupted him: "But, Theodore, you never told *me* to rest all day. I have been following you all day—" He laughed, but firmly said: "Sit right down here. You will be sorry if you go to bed. I am going to do something that is very interesting. William Rhodes has asked me to review his second and third volumes of the 'History of the United States.' You may have noticed I was reading those volumes on the way from Washington. I feel just like doing it now. The stenographer is rested, and as for you, it will do you a great deal of good, because you don't know as much as you should about American history." Smilingly he put me in a chair and began his dictation. Lord Morley is reported to have said, after his visit to the United States, when asked what he thought most interesting in our country: "There are two great things in the United States: one is Niagara, the other is Theodore

Roosevelt." As I think of my brother that night, Lord Morley's words come back to me, for it seemed as if, for once, the two great things were combined in one. Such a Niagara as flowed from the lips of Theodore Roosevelt would have surprised even the brilliant English statesman. He never once referred to the books themselves, but he ran through the whole gamut of their story, suggesting here, interpolating there, courteously referring to some slight inaccuracy, taking up occasionally almost a page of the matter (referring to the individual page without ever glancing at the book), and finally, at 5 A. M., with a satisfied aspect, he turned to me and said: "That is all about 'Rhodes's History.'"

I rose feebly to my feet and said: "Good night, darling." But not at all—still gaily, as if he had just begun a day's work, instead of having reached the weary, littered end of twenty-four hours, he said once more: "Don't go to bed. I must do one other piece of work, and I think you would be especially interested in it. Peter Dunne—'Dooley,' you know—has sent me an article of his on the Irish Question, and wants a review on that from me. I am very fond of Dunne, and really feel I should like to give him my opinions, as they do not entirely agree with his in this particular article. I feel like doing this now. Sit down again." He never asked me to do anything with him that I ever refused, were it in my power to assent to his suggestion. How I rejoice to think that this was the case, and there was no exception made to my usual rule at 5 A. M. that November morning. I sat down again, and sure enough, in a few moments all fatigue seemed to vanish from me, as I listened with eager interest to his masterly review of Peter Dunne's opinions on the Irish situation at that moment. It was a little late, or perhaps one might say a little early, to begin so complicated a subject as the Irish Question, and my final memories of his dictation are confused with the fact that at about 7 A. M. one of the colored porters came in with coffee, and shortly after that I was assisted to my berth in a more or less asphyxiated condition, from which I never roused again until the train reached the station at Washington. That was the way in which Theodore Roosevelt did work. I have often thought that if some of us always had the book at hand that we wanted to read, instead of wasting time in looking for it, if we always had clearly in our minds the extra job we wanted to do, and the tools at hand with which to do it, we might accomplish in some small degree the vast numbers of things he accomplished because of *preparedness*.

As early as December 19, 1904, my sister-in-law wrote me: "Theodore says that he wants you and Douglas under his roof for the Inauguration." I always felt a deep appreciation of the fact that both my brother and his wife made us so welcome at the most thrilling moments of their life in the White House.

In January, 1905, he came to stay with me in New York to speak at several dinners, and a most absurd and yet trying incident occurred, an incident which he met with his usual sunny and unselfish good humor. We had had a large luncheon for him at my home, and when the time came for him to dress in the evening for the dinner at which he was to speak, I suddenly heard a call from the third story, a pitiful call: "I don't think I have my own dress coat." I ran up-stairs, and sure enough the coat laid out with his evening clothes, when he tried to put it on, proved to be so tight across his broad shoulders that whenever he moved his hands it rose unexpectedly almost to his ears. I called my butler, who insisted that he had taken the President's coat with the rest of his clothes to brush, and had brought it back again to his room. This, however, was untrue, for the awful fact was soon divulged that the extra waiter engaged for the luncheon, and who had already left the house, had apparently confused the President's coat, which was in the basement to be pressed, with his own, and had taken away the President's coat! No one knew at this man's house where he had gone. There seemed no method of tracing the coat. We dressed my brother in my husband's coat, but that was even worse, for my husband's coat fell about him in folds, and there seemed nothing for it but to send him to the large public dinner with a coat that, unless most cleverly manipulated, continued to rise unexpectedly above his head. No one but my brother would have taken this catastrophe with unruffled gaiety, but he started off apparently perfectly contented, rather than give me a more dejected feeling than I already had about the misadventure. I, myself, was to go later to the dinner to hear his speech from one of the boxes, and I shall never forget my trepidation when he began his address, as I saw the coat slowly rising higher and higher. At the most critical moment, when it seemed about to surmount his head, a messenger-boy, flurried and flushed with exertion, ran upon the stage with a package in his hand. The recalcitrant waiter had been found by my butler, and the President's coat had been torn from his back. Excusing himself for a moment, with a laughing gesture which brought the coat completely over his head he retired into the wings, changed the article in question, and a few moments later brought down the whole house by his humorous account of the reason for his retirement.

On March 3, 1905, as the guests of my cousin Emlen

Roosevelt, who
took a special car
for the occasion,
the members of
my family, my
husband, and myself
started for the
inauguration of
Theodore Roosevelt
as President.
Memories crowd
about me of those
two or three days
at the White House.
The atmosphere was
one of great family

gaiety, combined with an underlying seriousness which showed the full realization felt by my brother of the great duties which he was again to assume this time as the choice of the people.

What a day it was, that inaugural day! As usual, the personal came so much into it. The night before, Mr. John Hay sent him a ring with a part of the lock of Abraham Lincoln's hair which John Hay himself had cut from the dead President's forehead almost immediately after his assassination. I have never known my brother to receive a gift for which he cared so deeply. To wear that ring on the day of his own inauguration as President of the United States, elected to the office by the free will of the great American people, was to him, perhaps, the highest fulfilment of his desires. The day dawned dark and threatening and with snow filtering through the clouds, but occasionally rifts of sunlight broke through the sombre bank of gray. The ceremonies were fraught, to those of us who loved him so deeply, with great solemnity. The Vice-President taking his oath in the senate-chamber, the arrival there of the judges of the Supreme Court, the glittering uniforms of the foreign ambassadors and their suites, the appearance of the President-elect, and our withdrawal to the porch of the Capitol, from which he was to make his inaugural address—all of this remains indelibly impressed upon my mind. His solemn, ardent words as he dedicated himself afresh to the service of the country, the great crowd straining to hear each sentence, the eager attitude of the guard of honor (his beloved Rough Riders)—all made a vivid picture never to be forgotten. An eye-witness wrote as follows: "Old Chief Justice Fuller with his beautiful white hair and his long, judicial gown administered the oath, and Roosevelt

repeated it so loudly
that he could be
heard in spite of
the wind. In fact the
wind rather added to
the impressiveness
than otherwise, as it
gave the President
a chance to throw
back his shoulders
to resist it, and that
gave you a wonderful
feeling of strength
that went splendidly
with the speech
itself. The speech

was short, and was mainly a plea for the 'Peace of Justice' as compared with the 'Peace of the Coward.' It was very stirring. The applause was tremendous."

I would have my readers remember that when Theodore Roosevelt pleaded for such a peace it was in 1905, nine years before peace was broken by the armies of the Huns, and during those long years he never once failed to preach that doctrine, and to the last moment of his life abhorred and denounced the peace of the coward.

Following quickly on his inaugural speech came the luncheon at the White House, at which friends from

New York were as cordially welcomed as were Bill Sewall's large family from the Maine woods and Will Merrifield, who, now a marshal, brought the greetings of the State of Montana. After luncheon we all went out on the reviewing-stand. The President stood at the front of the box, his hat always off in response to the salutes. The great procession lasted for hours—West Pointers and naval cadets followed by endless state organizations, governors on horseback, cowboys waving their lassos and shouting favorite slogans (they even lassoed a couple of men, en passant), Chief Joseph, the grand old man of the Nez Percé tribe, gorgeously caparisoned, his brilliant head-dress waving in the wind, followed by a body of Indians only a shade less superb in costume, and then a hundred and fifty Harvard fellows in black gowns and caps—and how they cheered for the President as they passed the stand! Surely there was never before such an inauguration of any President in Washington. Never was there such a feeling of personal devotion in so many hearts. Other Presidents have had equal admiration, equal loyalty perhaps, but none has had that loyalty and admiration given by so liberal and varied a number of his fellow countrymen.

It was dark before we left the stand, and soon inside of the White House there followed a reception to the Rough Riders. What a happy time the President had with them recalling bygone adventures, while the Roosevelt and Robinson children ran merrily about listening to the wonderful stories and feeding the voracious Rough Riders. Later the President went bareheaded to the steps under the porte-cochère and received the cowboys, who rode past one after another, joyfully shaking hands with their old chief, ready with some joke for his special benefit, to which there was always a repartee. It was a unique scene as they cheered the incoming magnate under the old porte-cochère, and one never to be repeated. And then the Harvard men filed past to shake hands. Needless to say, dinner was rather late, though very merry, and we were all soon off to the inaugural ball. It was a beautiful sight, the hall enormous, with two rows of arches and pillars, one above the other, along each side. The floor was absolutely crowded with moving people, all with their faces straining up at our box. Ten thousand people bought tickets. Mr. Matthew Hale, then tutor to my nephew

Theodore Roosevelt, Jr., has described the scene as follows: "The whole room was beautifully decorated with lights and wreaths and flowers. As I stood looking down on the great pageant I felt as though I were in some other world,—as though these people below there and moving in and out were not real

people, but were all
part of some great
mechanism built for
our special benefit.
And then my feeling
would change to
the other extreme
when I thought of
each one of those
men and women as
individuals, each one
thinking, and feeling
and acting according
to his own will,—
and that all, just
for that one night,

came together for a common purpose, to see the President. Soon an open place appeared in the throng before us, and the President and Mrs. Roosevelt, and behind them Vice-President and Mrs. Fairbanks, walked to the other end of the hall and back, while the people cheered and cheered." And soon it was time to go back to the White House, and then, best of all, came what we used to call a "back-hair" talk in Theodore and Edith's room. What fun we had as we talked the great day over in comfortable déshabille. A small round bottle of old wine was found somewhere by Mrs. Roosevelt, and the family drank the

President's health, and we talked of old times and childhood days, and of the dear ones whose hearts would have glowed so warmly had they lived to see that day. We laughed immoderately over all kinds of humorous happenings, and we could hardly bear to say "good night," we still felt so gay, so full of life and fun, so invigorated and stimulated by the excitement and by the deeper thoughts and desires, which, however, only took the form that night of increasing hilarity!

Shortly after that March inauguration my daughter Corinne, just eighteen, was asked by her kind aunt to pay a visit at the White House, and I impressed upon her the wonderful opportunity she would have of listening to the great men of the world at the informal luncheon gatherings which were a feature of my brother's incumbency. "Do not miss a word," I said to my daughter. "Uncle Ted brings to luncheon all the great men in Washington— almost always several members of the cabinet, and any one of interest who is visiting there. Be sure and listen to everything. You will never hear such talk again." When she returned home from that visit I eagerly asked her about the wonderful luncheons at the White House, where I had so frequently sat spellbound. My somewhat irreverent young daughter said: "Mother, I laughed internally all through the first luncheon at the White House during my visit. Uncle Ted was perfectly lovely to me, and took me by the hand and said: 'Corinny, dear, you are to sit at my right hand to-day, and you must have the most delightful person in

the room on your
other side.' With that
he glanced at the
distinguished crowd
of gentlemen who
were surrounding
him waiting to be
assigned to their
places, and picking
out a very elderly
gentleman with a
long white beard,
he said with glowing
enthusiasm: 'You
shall have John
Burroughs, the

great naturalist.' I confess I had hoped for some secretary in the cabinet, but, no, Uncle Ted did not think there was any one in the world that compared in thrilling excitement to his wonderful old friend and lover of birds. Even so, I thought, 'Mother would wish me to learn all about natural history, and I shall hear marvellous ornithological tales, even if politics must be put aside.' But even in that I was somewhat disappointed, for at the very beginning of luncheon Uncle Ted leaned across me to Mr. Burroughs and said: 'John, this morning I heard a chippy sparrow, and he sang twee, twee, right in my ear.' Mr. Burroughs, with a shade of disapproval on his face, said: 'Mr. President, you must be mistaken. It was not a chippy sparrow if it sang twee, twee. The note of the chippy sparrow is twee, twee, twee.' From that moment the great affairs of our continent, the international crises of all kinds were utterly forgotten, while the President of the United States and his esteemed guest, the great naturalist, discussed with a good deal of asperity whether that chippy sparrow had said 'twee, twee,' or 'twee, twee, twee.' We rose from the table with the question still unsettled." My brother always loved to hear my daughter tell this story, although his face would assume a somewhat sheepish expression as she dilated on the difference between her mother's prognostications of what a luncheon at the White House would mean from an intellectual standpoint, and what the realization actually became!

In spite of my daughter's experience, however, I can say with truth that there never were such luncheons as those luncheons at the White House during my brother's life there. The secretary of state, Mr. Elihu Root, with his unusual knowledge, his pregnant wit, and quiet, brilliant sarcasm; the secretary of war, Mr. Taft, with his gay smile and ready response; Mr. Moody, the attorney-general with his charming culture and universal kindliness, and Senator Henry Cabot Lodge, the brilliant scholar and statesman, my brother's most intimate friend and constant companion,

were frequent
members of the
luncheon-parties,
and always, the most
distinguished visitor
to Washington, from
whatever country
or from whatever
State of our own
country, would be
brought in with
the same informal
hospitality and
received for the time
being by President
and Mrs. Roosevelt

into the intimacy of family life. The whole cabinet would occasionally adjourn from one of their most important meetings to the lunch-table, and then the President and Mr. Root would cap each other's stories of the way in which this or that question had been discussed during the cabinet meeting. I doubt also

if ever there were
quite such cabinet
meetings as were
held during those
same years!

That spring Mr.
Robinson and I took
my daughter to Porto
Rico to visit Governor
and Mrs. Beekman
Winthrop. My brother
believed strongly
in young men, and
having admired the
intelligence of young

Beekman Winthrop (he came of a fine old New York family) as circuit judge in the Philippines, he decided to make him governor of Porto Rico. He was only twenty-nine, and his charming wife still younger, but they made a most ideal couple as administrators of the beautiful island. After having been with them in the old palace for about a week, and having enjoyed beyond measure all that was so graciously arranged for us, I was approached one day by Governor Winthrop, who told me that he was much distressed at the behavior of a certain official and that he felt sure that the President would not wish the man to remain in office, for he was actually a disgrace to the United States. "Mrs. Robinson," he said, "will you not go to the President on your return, and tell him that I am quite sure he would not wish to retain this man in office? I know the President likes us to work with the tools which have been given us, and I dislike beyond measure to seem not to be able to do so, but I am convinced that this man should not represent the United States in this island." "Have you your proofs, Beekman?" I asked. "I should not be willing to approach my brother with any such criticism without accurate proofs." "I most assuredly have them," he answered, and sure enough he did have them, and I shortly afterward sailed with them back to New York. Immediately upon my arrival I telegraphed my brother as follows: "Would like to see you on Porto Rican business. When shall I come?" One of Theodore Roosevelt's most striking characteristics was the rapidity with which he answered letters or telegrams. One literally felt that one had not posted a letter or sent the telegram rushing along the wire before the rapid answer came winging back again, and that particular telegram was no exception to the rule. I had rather hoped for a week's quiet in which to get settled after my trip to Porto Rico, but that was not to be. The rapid-fire answer read as follows: "Come tomorrow." Of course there was nothing for me to do but go "tomorrow." It was late in April, and as I drove up to the White House from the station, I thought how lovely a city was Washington in the springtime. The yellow forsythias gave a golden glow to the squares, and the soft hanging petals of the fringe-trees waved in the scented air. I never drove under the White House porte-cochère without a romantic feeling of excitement at the realization that it was my brother, lover of Lincoln, lover of

America, who lived under the roof which symbolized all that America means to her children. As I went up the White House steps, he blew out of the door, dressed for his ride on horseback. His horse and that of a companion were waiting for him. He came smilingly toward me, welcomed me, and said: "Edie has had to go to

Philadelphia for the night to visit Nellie Tyler, so we are all alone, and I have ordered dinner out on the back porch, for it is so warm and lovely, and there is a full moon, and I thought we could be so quiet there. I have so much to tell you. All sorts of political things have happened during your absence, and besides that I have learned several new poems of Kipling and Swinburne, and I feel like reciting them to you in the moonlight!" "How perfectly lovely," I replied, "and when shall I see you about Porto Rico?" A slight frown came on his brow, and he said, "Certainly not to-night," and then rather sternly: "You have your appointment at nine o'clock to-morrow morning in the office to discuss business matters." Then with a returning smile: "I will be back pretty soon. Good-by." And he jumped on his horse and clattered away toward Rock Creek.

It all came true, although it almost seemed like a

fairy-tale. We had that dinner à deux on the lovely portico at the rear of the White House looking toward the Washington Monument—
that portico was beautifully reproduced by Sargent's able brush for Mrs. Roosevelt later—and under the great, soft moon, with the scent of shrub and

flower in the air,
he recited Kipling
and Swinburne, and
then falling into
more serious vein,
gave me a vivid
description of some
difficulty he had
had with Congress,
which had refused
to receive a certain
message which he
had written and
during the interval
between the sending
of it and their final

decision to receive it, he had shut himself up in his library, glad to have a moment of unexpected leisure, and had written an essay, which he had long desired to write, on the Irish sagas. The moon had waned and the stars were brighter and deeper before we left the portico. We never could go to bed when we were together, and I am so glad that we never did!

The next morning I knocked at his door at eight o'clock, to go down to the early breakfast with the children, which was one of the features also, quite as much as were the brilliant lunches, of home life in the White House. He came out of his dressing-room radiant and smiling, ready for the day's work, looking as if he had had eight hours of sleep instead of five, and rippling all over with the laughter which he always infused into those family breakfasts. As we passed the table at the head of the staircase, at which later in the day my sister's secretary wrote her letters, the telephone-bell on the table rang, and with spontaneous simplicity—not even thinking of ringing a bell for a "menial" to answer the telephone-call—he picked up the receiver himself as he passed by. His face assumed a listening look, and then a broad smile broke over his features. "No," he said. "No, I am not Archie, I am Archie's father." A second passed and he laughed aloud, and then said: "All right, I will tell him; I won't forget." Hanging up the receiver, he turned to me half-sheepishly but very much amused. "That's a good joke on any President," he said. "You may have realized that there was a little boy on the other end of that wire, and he started the conversation by saying, 'Is that you, Archie?' and I replied, 'No, it is Archie's father.' Whereupon he answered, with evident disgust: 'Well, you'll do. Be sure and tell Archie to come to supper. Now, don't forget.' 'How the creatures order you about!'" he gaily quoted from our favorite book, "Alice in Wonderland," and proceeded to run at full speed down to the breakfast-room. There the children greeted us vociferously, and the usual merry breakfast ensued. For that half-hour he always belonged to the children. Questions and answers about their school life, their recreation when out of school, etc., etc., followed in rapid succession, interspersed with various fascinating tales told by him for their special edification.

After they had dispersed there was still a half-hour left before he went to the office at 9 o'clock, and whenever I visited the White House (my visits were rather rare, as my husband, being a busy real-estate broker in New York, could not often break away) that half-hour was always given to me, and we invariably walked around the great circle at the back of the White House. It was his most vigorous moment of the day, that hour from 8.30 to 9. He had not yet met the puzzling defeats and compromises necessitated by the conflicting interests of the many appointments in the office, and he was fresh and vivid, interested in the problems that were to be brought to him for solution that day, and observant of everything around him. I remember that morning as we walked around the circle he was discussing a very serious problem that had to be decided immediately, and he held his forefinger straight up, and said: "You know my temperament always wants to get there"—putting his other forefinger on the apex of the first. "I naturally wish to reach the goal of my desire, but would I not be very blind and stupid if, because I couldn't get there, I decided to stay here" [changing his right forefinger to the base of the left] "rather than get here"—finishing his simile by placing the right finger to the third notch of the finger on his other hand.

Just as he was finishing this simile his eye caught sight of a tiny object on the pathway, so minute a little brown spot that I should never have noticed it; but he stooped, picked it up, and held it between his forefinger and thumb, looking at it eagerly, and then muttering somewhat below his breath: "Very early for a fox-sparrow." He threw the tiny piece of fluff again upon the path. "How do you know that that was a feather from a fox-sparrow, Theodore?" I said, in my usual astonishment at his observation and information. "I can understand how you

might know it was
a sparrow, but how
know it belonged
to the fox-sparrow
rather than to any of
the other innumerable
little creatures of
that species?" He was
almost deprecatory
in his manner as he
said in reply: "Well,
you see I have really
made a great study
of sparrows." And
then we were back at
the entrance to the

White House, and in a moment I leaned out of the dining-room window and watched him walk across the short space between that window and the office, his head thrown back, his shoulders squared to meet the difficulties of the day, and every bit of him alert, alive, and glowing with health and strength and power and mentality.

I went up-stairs, put on my "best bib and tucker," and proceeded to go around the other way to the front door of the offices. As I rang the bell the dear old man who always opened the door greeted me warmly, and said: "Yes, Mrs. Douglas Robinson, your appointment is

at 9. It is just time."
I went into the outer
hall, where a number
of the appointees of
9.15, 9.30, etc., were
already waiting, to
be surely on hand for
their appointments,
and in a moment or
two Mr. Loeb opened
the door of the
private office of the
President, and came
out into the hall
and said in a rather
impersonal way, "Mrs.

Douglas Robinson's appointment," and I was shown into the room. My brother was seated at a large table, and on it was every imaginable paper marked "Porto Rico." As I entered he was still reading one of these papers. He looked up, and I almost felt a shock as I met what seemed to be a pair of perfectly opaque blue eyes. I could hardly believe they were the eyes of the brother with whom I had so lately parted, the eyes that had glistened as he recited the poems of Kipling and Swinburne, the eyes that had almost closed to see better the tiny breast-fluff of the fox-sparrow. These were rather cold eyes, the eyes

of a just judge, eyes
that were turned
upon his sister as
they would have
been turned upon
any other individual
who came to him
in connection with
a question about
which he must give
his most careful and
deliberate decision.
He waved me to a
chair, finished the
paper he was reading,
and then turning to

me, his eyes still stern and opaque, he said: "I believe you have come to see me on business connected with Porto Rico. Kindly be as condensed as possible." I decided to meet him on his own ground, and made my eyes as much like his as possible, and was as condensed as possible. Having listened carefully to my short story, he said: "Have you proof of this?" still rather sternly. Again I decided to answer as he asked, and I replied: "I should not be here, wasting your time and mine, did I not have adequate proof." With that I handed him the notes made by the governor of Porto Rico, and proceeded to explain them. He became a little less severe after reading them, but no less serious, and turning to me more gently, said: "This is a very serious matter. I have got to be sure of the correctness of these statements. A man's whole future hangs upon my decision." For a moment I felt like an executioner, but realizing as I did the shocking and disgraceful behavior of the official in question, I knew that no sentimentality on my part should interfere with the important decision to be made, and I briefly backed up all that the governor had written. I can still hear the sound of the President's pen as he took out the paper on which the man's name was inscribed, and with one strong stroke effaced that name from official connection with Porto Rico forever. That was the way that Theodore Roosevelt did business with his sister.

During that same year, 1905, the old Provençal poet Frédéric Mistral sent him his volume called

"Mireille," and the acknowledgment of the book seems to me to express more than almost any other letter ever written by my brother the spirit which permeated his whole life. It shows indisputably that though he had reached the apex of his desires, that though he was a great President of a great country, perhaps the most powerful ruler at the moment of any country, that his ideals for that country, just as his ideals for himself and for his own beloved home life, were what they had always been before the sceptre of power had been clasped by his outstretched hand.

White House,
Washington,

December 15, 1905.

My dear M. Mistral:

Mrs. Roosevelt and I were equally pleased with the book and the medal, and none the less because for nearly twenty years we have possessed a copy of Mireille. That copy we shall keep for old association's sake, though this new copy with the personal inscription by you must hereafter occupy the place of honor.

All success to you and your associates! You are teaching the lesson that none need more to learn than we of the West, we of the eager, restless, wealth-seeking nation; the

lesson that after
a certain not very
high level of material
well-being has been
reached, then the
things that really
count in life are
the things of the
spirit. Factories and
railways are good up
to a certain point,
but courage and
endurance, love of
wife and child, love
of home and country,
love of lover for

sweetheart, love
of beauty in man's
work and in nature,
love and emulation
of daring and of
lofty endeavour, the
homely work-a-day
virtues and the
heroic virtues—these
are better still, and
if they are lacking,
no piled-up riches,
no roaring, clanging
industrialism,
no feverish and
many-sided activity

shall avail either the individual or the nation. I do not undervalue these things of a nation's body; I only desire that they shall not make us forget that beside the nation's body there is also the nation's soul.

Again thanking you on behalf of both of us, believe me,

Faithfully yours,

(Signed)   Theodore
Roosevelt.

No wonder that
Mistral turned to a
friend after reading
that letter and said
with emotion: "It is
he who is the new
hope of humanity."

Men smile through
falling tears,

Remembering the
courage of his years

That stood each one
for God, humanity,

And covenanted
world-wide Liberty!

—Edith Daley.

PART TWO

One of the most
extraordinary things
about my brother was
that in the midst of
his full political life,
a life "pressed down
and overflowing," he
still had time for the
most loving interest
in personal family
matters. Just after
the great moment of
his inauguration, he
sent me a number

of photographs of my eldest son and his young wife, just married, who had gone around the world and were staying with General Wood in the Philippines, and adds in the letter: "It was such a pleasure to have Douglas and you down here for the inauguration, and to see the boys and Corinne." In June of that same year, when my two younger boys had each won a boat-race at St. Paul's School, he takes a moment from his pressing duties to write another letter: "Darling Corinne: Good for Monroe and Stewart! Give them my hearty congratulations; I have only time for this line." Such unusual thoughtfulness could not fail to keep burning perpetually the steady fire of my love for him.

In July, 1905, he sent me one of the inauguration medals signed by Saint-Gaudens. In looking at the head upon that medal, one realized perfectly by the strong lines of temple and forehead that Theodore Roosevelt had come to the fulness of his intellectual powers.

About the same time there was a naval review at Oyster Bay, and Mrs. Roosevelt writes: "The review was a wonderful sight. I wish you could have been here. The morning was dark and stormy, with showers of driving rain, until Theodore's flag broke out from the Mayflower, when the clouds suddenly dispersed and the sun shone brightly." How often we used to feel that the sun always broke out when Theodore's flag flew!

One other little line from his pen, December 19, 1905, shows the same constant thoughtfulness. He says: "Will you send the enclosed note to Dora? I am not sure of her address. I hate to trouble you, but I want to have poor 'Dolly' get it by Christmas Day." Dora was his old, childhood nurse, one to whom we were very much devoted, and whom he never forgot.

At the beginning of the new year, 1906, he writes to my husband: "Dear Douglas,—By George! Stewart is doing well. [I think this referred to the fact that my youngest boy had been chosen as goal-keeper of the St. Paul's School hockey team!] That is awfully nice. I was mighty glad Wadsworth was elected. I shall have difficulties this year, and I cannot expect to get along as well as I did last year, but I shall do the best I can." Never blinded by past popularity, always ready for the difficulties to come, and yet never dwelling so strongly on these difficulties that by the very dwelling on them even greater difficulties were brought to bear upon him. It was quite true that it proved in many ways, a more difficult year than the one preceding, but a happy year all the same, a happiness which culminated in his satisfaction in the marriage of his daughter Alice to Nicholas Longworth, of Cincinnati, Ohio,

an able member
of the House of
Representatives. His
announcement to me
of the engagement
was made at the
dinner-table one
evening before it was
known to the world,
and not wishing to
have it disclosed to
the world through
the table-servants,
he decided to give
me the news in
French. His French

was always fluent, but more or less of a literal translation from the English, which method he exaggerated humorously. "Je vais avoir un fils en loi," he said, smiling gaily at me across the table, delighted at my puzzled expression. With a little more explanation I realized what he was suggesting to my befuddled brain, and he then proceeded to describe a conversation he had had with the so-called "fils en loi," and how he had talked to him like "un oncle Hollandais," or "Dutch uncle"!

There was much excitement at the prospect of a wedding in the White

House, and, needless to say, so many were the requests to be present that the line had to be drawn very carefully, and, in consequence, the whole affair assumed an intimate and personal aspect. Alice's Boston grandparents, Mr. and Mrs. George C. Lee, were especially welcomed by Mrs. Roosevelt, and my memory of the great morning of the wedding has a curiously "homey" quality. I much doubt if there was ever a function—for a wedding in the White House could hardly be anything but a function—so simple, so charming, and so informal as that marriage of the lovely daughter of the White

House. Almost all the morning Mrs. Roosevelt knitted peacefully at the sunny window up-stairs near her secretary's desk, chatting quietly with Mrs. Lee. All preparations seemed to have been made in, the most quiet and efficient manner, for there was no hurry, no excitement. My husband took

Mr. Lee for a walk, as the dear old gentleman was very much excited at the prospect of his granddaughter's nuptials in the "East Room." Everything seemed to go on quite as usual until the actual moment came, and Alice Roosevelt, looking very beautiful in her long court train and graceful veil, came through the group of interested friends up to the white ribbon which formed, with flowers, a chancel at the end of the "East Room." My brother was at his best— gay, affectionate, full of life and fun, and later took his son-in-law (no longer "to-be") and all the ushers, members of Harvard's Porcellian Club like himself, into the state dining-room to drink the health of the bride and groom, and recall various incidents of his and of their college days.

In March of that year I wrote him that my youngest boy was to debate at St. Paul's School on the Santo Domingo question, and he answered at once, with that marvellous punctuality of his: "I wrote Stewart at once and sent him all the information I could on the Santo Domingo business. I wish you were down here. In great haste. Ever yours, T. R."

In great haste, yes, but not too busy to write to a schoolboy-nephew "at once," and give him the most accurate information that could be given on the question upon which he was to take part in school debate.

Again, when I suggested joining him in his car on his way that fall to vote at Oyster Bay, he writes: "Three cheers! Now you can join me. We will have lunch immediately after leaving. I am so anxious to see you. I shall just love the Longfellow." [Evidently some special edition that I am about to bring to him.]

On November 20, with his usual interest in my boys, he sends me a delightful letter from his ex-cowboy superintendent, Will Merrifield, with whom they had been hunting in August and September, 1906; and I am interested to see after reading his opinion of my boys how Mr. Merrifield, although many years had passed since the old days of the Elkhorn Ranch, still turns to him for advice, still, beyond all else, wishes to justify his various ventures in the eyes of his old "boss." Merrifield writes: "I have sold my ranch, and will be able to make good all my financial obligations, which was my great ambition, besides having something left, so that I will not take office for the purpose of making money. [That was one of Theodore Roosevelt's perpetual preachings, that no one should take office for the purpose of making money.] I can be independent as far as money goes, and above all will be able to make good my word to you years ago, as soon as my business is straightened out." He sends me the letter not because of that sentence, but because, as he says, "This letter from Merrifield is so nice about Monroe and Stewart that I thought I would send it to you. How well they did." Always the same generous joy in the achievements of any of the younger generation.

Again, on December 26, comes a long letter describing another "White House Christmas."

He deplores the fact that the children are growing a little older, and that "Ted" says in a melancholy way that he no longer feels the wild excitement of former years and the utter inability to sleep soundly during the night before Christmas. He adds, however: "Personally I think that 'Ted' also was thoroughly in the spirit of the thing when Christmas actually arrived, because by six o'clock every child of every size was running violently to and fro along the hall, in and out of all the other children's rooms, the theory being that Edith and I were still steeped in dreamless and undisturbed slumber!"

It is true that that winter was more difficult than the winter before, but he met the unusual difficulties with unabated courage, and writes in October, 1907, after giving me much family news: "Indeed times have been bad in New York, and as is always the case the atonement was largely vicarious, and innocent people suffered. I hope it does not extend through the rest of the country. If we check it, I think it will mean ultimate good, though it will also mean depression for a year at least."

In March, 1908, in the midst of harassing controversies and presidential difficulties of all kinds, he takes the time and interest to write concerning a young friend of mine into whose life had come an unfortunate trouble. The letter is so full of a certain quality—what perhaps I might call a righteous ruthlessness specially characteristic of Theodore Roosevelt—that I quote a few lines from it:

"I hate to think of her suffering; but the only thing for her to do now is to treat the past as past, the event as finished and out of her life; to dwell on it, and above all to keep talking of it with any one, would be both weak and morbid. She should try not to think of it; this she cannot wholly avoid, but she can avoid speaking of it. She should show a brave and cheerful front to the world, whatever she feels; and henceforth she should never speak one word of the matter to any one. In the long future, when the memory is too dead to throb, she may, if she wishes, speak of it once more, but if she is wise and brave, she will not speak of it now."

This note referring to a matter which did not come, except through the interests of affection, close to his own life shows with startling clearness the philosophy of his attitude toward sorrows wherein an original mistake had perhaps been the cause of sorrow. Of all the qualities in my brother, this one never failed him. It was not harshness; it was, as I said, a righteous ruthlessness. The thing that injured one's possibility for service in any way must be cut out or burnt out. When that great sorrow of his own life, the death of his splendid boy, came in July, 1918, although he never put aside the sympathy of others—indeed, he gladly welcomed it, and gladly even would talk with those in his innermost circle of the youngest he loved so well—still, as a rule, his attitude was similar to that taken in the above letter. Morbid craving could not bring back his child; morbid craving could hurt his own potential power for good. The grief must be met with high head and squared shoulders, and the work still to do must be done.

All through the spring of 1908 the question as to his successor in the White House was constantly in his mind. After serious thought he had come to the conclusion that of the men closest to him, William Howard Taft, who had done splendid work as governor in the Philippines and had been an able lieutenant in the work of the Roosevelt administration, would most conscientiously carry out the policies he thought vital for the country. This belief did not in any way mean that he wished Mr. Taft to be an automaton or dummy, possible of manipulation, but he felt that his then secretary of war was more thoroughly in sympathy with the policies which he believed to be the right policies for our country than any other man except the secretary of state, Mr. Elihu Root, whose possible election to the presidency he felt would be very doubtful. Many have criticised in later years, especially after the trouble in 1912, his choice of Mr. Taft to succeed him. There came out at one time an article in the periodical Life which, to my mind, explained well the confidence which my brother placed in almost every man who worked with him. The article said approximately: "The reason that Theodore Roosevelt occasionally made mistakes in feeling that some of his associates in the work of the government would continue to be what

he believed them
to be, is as follows:
While any individual
was working with Mr.
Roosevelt, in fact,
under Mr. Roosevelt,
the latter had the
power of inspiring the
said individual with
his own acuteness,
his own energy, his
own ability. The
person, therefore,
frequently shone
with a reflex light, a
light which seemed

to Mr. Roosevelt to originate in him, but in fact, came from his own unfailing sources. The consequence is that when some official who had seemed to Mr. Roosevelt to be almost a rara avis, was left to his own devices, and without the magnetic personality of his chief to inspire in him qualities not really indigenous in him, the change in what that official could accomplish was very marked." Theodore Roosevelt was convinced that Mr. Taft was entirely in accord with the policies in which he so fully believed, and he had absolute confidence that in leaving in his hands the work which he had striven so hard to perfect, he was doing the best thing possible for the United States.

At that time the people wanted to renominate my brother as President. He, however, was convinced that a renomination would have defeated the spirit of the unwritten law that no man should succeed himself a third time in succession.

I was present at the convention in Chicago in 1908, and have fortunately retained a letter written to my children the very morning of that convention, which runs as follows:

"Oh, how I wish you could have been here this morning. Such an ovation was never known as greeted Mr. Lodge's mention of your Uncle Ted. Mr. Lodge's speech was most scholarly and reserved, and in referring to the laws, he said, 'The President has invariably enforced the laws, and the President is the most abused and the most popular man in the country.' Then came a ripple and then a mighty shout of applause, growing louder and louder, increasing and increasing more and more every moment. They clapped, they shouted, they cheered. The whole great Convention sang the Star Spangled Banner, and then they clapped again, and carried 'Teddybears' around the hall. They took off their coats and swung them around their heads. You have never even imagined anything like it. Several times, Mr. Lodge raised his gavel, but with no result, and finally he started his speech again, and persevered until the deafening noise began to subside fifty minutes after it began. It really was a wonderful and thrilling scene. It was three o'clock before we could keep our luncheon engagement at George Porter's that first day."

The following day it required all Mr. Lodge's determination, and a ringing message over the telephone from the White House itself, to prevent the renomination of my brother. Not only did the people want him, but, what has been so often not the case, the delegates wanted him as well. It was one of those rare moments at a great convention when the people and the delegates were in accord, and yet, it was not to be. The will of Theodore Roosevelt

was carried out,
and William Howard
Taft was chosen as
the nominee of the
Republican party for
the next President of
the United States.

On June 23, 1908,
came a letter from
the White House
to me: "Darling
Corinne—It was
very good of you
and Douglas to
telegraph me. I am

extremely pleased with the result of the Convention. I think Cabot's handling of it was masterly." And then, on June 26, an extremely interesting letter came, one, I think, which, written as it was four years before the great controversy of 1912, settles forever that question which was so much discussed as to what Theodore

Roosevelt meant by his statement that he would not run for the presidency again. This letter, on White House paper, is dated Oyster Bay, June 26, 1908:

"Darling Corinne—My letter must have crossed yours. It was just exactly as you and Alice said. Now there is nothing to explain. I have been much amused at the fact that my English friends are wholly incapable of understanding my reasons for the view I take, and think it due to weakness or some fantastic scruple on my part. My theory has been that the presidency should be a powerful office, and the President a powerful man, who will take every advantage of it; but, as a corollary, a man who can be held accountable to the people, after a term of four years, and who will not in any event occupy it for more than a stretch of eight years...." Nothing is more conclusive of my brother's attitude than that sentence "who will not in any event occupy it for

more than a stretch
of eight years."
He did not believe
in a third term
consecutively, but in
no way did he pledge
himself at that time,
or at any other
time, not to consider
again the possible
gift of the highest
place in the nation,
should an interval
come between his
occupancy of the
White House and

the renewed desire
of the people that
he should fill that
place in the nation
once more. I have
given some time
to his attitude on
this question, as
it has been much
misunderstood.

In amusing contrast
to the seriousness
of his decision
not to accept a
renomination comes a

characteristic incident in the President's career. The account of this I quote from a letter to me of Mr. Gustavus Town Kirby, a participator himself in the event. The letter runs as follows:

"In 1908 the Olympic Games had been held at London, England, and when the athletes returned to this country, most of them went, with some heads of the American Olympic Committee, including the late James E. Sullivan and myself, to visit and receive the congratulations of the then President of the United States at his summer home in Oyster Bay. [What committee, on no matter what important business, did not receive the

congratulations
of that eclectic
President at his
summer home
at Oyster Bay!] I
shall never forget
the enthusiasm of
the gathering, nor
how, no sooner had
either Sullivan or I
presented a member
of the team to the
President, than he
would, by use of his
wonderful memory
and in his most

inspiring manner, tell the special athlete all about his own performance,—how far he had put the shot to win his event, or how gamely he had run; by how much he had beaten his competitor; his new world-record time, and the like. At the time I marvelled, and I thought even one as great as he must have 'brushed up' for the occasion, but 'Billy' Loeb, his Secretary, told me afterwards that it was not so, and that all during the Games he was kept constantly informed of the result of the performances of our boys; and while he actually knew none of these boys by sight, he not only knew them by name, but their performances as well. Not only to me, but to all gathered at this reception was this feat of memory most astounding. Mr. Roosevelt's gracious cordiality, his fine speech of congratulation, and his magnetic personality had such an effect on all that it was with great difficulty that they could be literally driven from the grounds and onto the Long Island boat for their return to New York.

"Michael Murphy, the trainer, many years trainer at Yale, and thereafter at 'Pennsylvania,' and also for the New York Athletic Club, whose team in 1895 was triumphant over the great team of the

London Athletic Club, was also a member of the party. On the way back in the boat I happened to pass through the cabin, which was entirely empty except for Michael Murphy, who, like the all but wizened-up old man he was, having but about a quarter of a lung, and deaf except to those things which he could not hear, sat huddled in a corner. I went up to Mike and said, 'What are you doing?' He answered, 'I am thinking!' I replied, 'Yes, that is evident; but what are you thinking about?' He then said: 'Well, Mr. Kirby, I suppose there is no doubt but that I am the greatest trainer of men in the world.' 'That certainly is true,' I said. He went on: 'Mr. Kirby, you are all wrong; until we went down to Oyster Bay I thought I might be, but now I know I am not.' 'But,' I said, 'Mike, that is nonsense. What do you mean?' Then Mike answered, 'Give me sixty men, every one of whom is a champion, and let that man at Oyster Bay have sixty other men, every one of whom is a dub, and his team would lick mine every time!' I said, 'Mike, this is impossible; it could not be,' and then Mike continued,— showing how that magnetic personality of Mr. Roosevelt's had taken hold of him, and how truly he, Mike Murphy, understood the psychology of inspiration,—'Yes, Mr.

Kirby, you see it's this way; that man down there would tell a miler that he could reel off a mile in four minutes, (as you know, no one has run, or ever will run a mile in four minutes) and not only would that man think he could run a mile in four minutes, but, by Gad, he'd go out and do it.'"

Perhaps no one has ever more cleverly expressed the extraordinary power of that personality than that wizened old trainer, sunk into despondency because he realized that where men are concerned skill and science are as nothing compared to the genius of leadership.

That summer my brother showed to my husband and myself his never-failing love and consideration in a very special manner. My husband's mother had died a couple of years before, and her son and daughter and myself had decided that the most fitting memorial to one who was specially beloved and missed in the immediate vicinity of her old home would be the erection of a small free library to the memory of her and her husband. The building was completed, and my husband wished to have a dedication service, at which time he would hand over the keys to the library trustees in our village of Jordanville. My

husband's old home,
a grant in the time
of Queen Anne to his
great-great-great-
grandfather, Doctor
James Henderson,
of Scotland, had
always been a place
for which my brother
had a deep affection.
Situated as it was
on the high Mohawk
hills overlooking
the great sweep of
typical American
farm-land, we lived a

somewhat Scotch life in the old gray-stone mansion copied from the manor-house of Mr. Robinson's Scotch ancestors. My brother delighted in our relationship with the neighbors in our environment, and accepted gladly my husband's earnest desire that he should make the speech of dedication when the library was given by us to the little village of Jordanville.

It was a great day for that tiny village when the President of the United States, his secretary of state, Mr. Elihu Root, and the Vice-President-elect, James S. Sherman, a native of the next county, after being our guests at luncheon, proceeded on my husband's four-in-hand brake to the steps of the little colonial building three miles away, designed by our friend Mr. S. Breck P. Trowbridge.

What a day it was and what fun we had! After the library exercises we held a reception at our home, Henderson House, and hundreds of every sort and

kind of vehicle were
left or tethered
along the high ridge
near our house.
My brother and I
stood at the end
of the quaint old
drawing-room, and
an endless file of
country neighbors
passed before him,
and each and all
were greeted with his
personal enthusiasm
and the marvellous
knowledge of their

interests with which the slightest word from me seemed to make him cognizant. The sunset lights faded over the Mohawk hills and lost their last gleam in the winding river below before the last "dead-wood coach" or broken-down buggy had disappeared from the grounds of Henderson House, and then in the old hall my own family servants—many of them had been twenty or thirty years upon the place—came in to greet him after supper, and sang the hymn which they often sang on Sunday evenings: "God be with you till we meet again." The stories of that day will be told in time to come by the children's

children of my kind
friends of Warren
Township, Herkimer
County. Theodore
himself writes of
the experience as
follows:

"Oyster Bay, August
27, 1908. Dearest
Corinne and Douglas:
There is not a thing
I would have missed
throughout the
whole day. It was
a very touching

little ceremony, and
most of all it was
delightful to see you
two in your lovely
home, living just
the kind of life that
I feel is typical of
what American life
should be at its best.
I was so glad to see
all your neighbors,
and to see the terms
they were on with
you. Moreover, the
view, the grounds,
the house itself, and

all there was therein,
were delightful
beyond measure; and
most delightful of
all was it to see the
three generations
ranging from you two
to the babies of dear
Helen and Teddy.
Ever yours, Theodore
Roosevelt." As usual,
he never spared
an effort to do the
lovely thing, and then
say the satisfying
thing to those for

whom he had done the service.

And now the time of Theodore Roosevelts incumbency as President was drawing to a close. There is always a glamour as well as a shadow over "last times," and my last visit to the White House, in February, 1909, stands out very clearly. My brother, the year before, had sent the great American fleet around the world, an expedition discountenanced by many, and yet conceded later to have been one of his most brilliantly conceived strategic inspirations. "In time of peace, prepare for war," said Washington, and Theodore Roosevelt always followed that maxim. That trip around the world of the American fleet was more conducive to peace than any other action that could have been taken. The purpose was "friendly," of course, but those splendid battle-ships of ours, engineered by such able commanders, could not fail to be an object-lesson to any who felt that the United States was too isolated to care for her own defense.

But even in such a demonstration as this, he managed to include a touch of exquisite sentiment. When the great vessels neared the Hawaiian Islands, he ordered them to deflect their course to pass by and salute the tragic island of Molokai, home of the afflicted lepers, so that they too should know of the protection which America affords to its most unfortunate children.

During those days in February, 1909, he seemed as gay as a boy let out of school. He was making all the arrangements for his great African adventure. In fact, with his usual "preparedness," he had been preparing for that event for a whole year. Everything was accurately arranged, and he and his son Kermit were to start immediately after he was to leave the White House in March. The lectures

which he was to
deliver a year from
the following spring
were all written
and corrected. One
afternoon in the
"Blue Bedroom,"
which I generally
occupied on my
visits, I heard a
knock at my door,
and he came in with
several rolls of paper
under his arm. "It
is raining," he said,
"and I think I won't

take my ride. I want your opinion on the lectures I am to deliver at Oxford, in Berlin, and at the Sorbonne. I should like to read them to you," and we settled down for a long delightful, quiet time "à deux." As usual, he was more than willing to listen to any remark or criticism, and once or twice accepted my slight suggestions of what I thought could improve his articles.

Some people felt that my brother was often egotistical, and mistook his conviction that this or that thing was right for an egotistical inability to look at it any other way. When he was convinced that his own attitude was correct, and that for the good of this or that scheme no other attitude should be taken, then nothing could swerve him; but when, as was often the case, it was not a question of conviction, but of advisability, he was the most open-minded of men, and gladly accepted and pondered the point of view of

any one in whom
he had confidence. I
was always touched
and gratified
beyond measure
at the simple and
sometimes almost
humble way in which
he would listen
to a difference of
opinion upon my
part. Occasionally,
after thinking it
seriously over, he
would concede that
my point of view

was right. In this particular case, however, they were the slightest of slight suggestions which I made, for each of those articles seemed to me in its own way a masterpiece.

During that visit also occurred the last diplomatic dinner, always followed when he was President by the delightful,

informal supper
at tables set in
the upper hall of
the White House.
That night he was
particularly gay,
and many witty
repartees passed
between him and our
beautiful and gifted
friend, Mrs. Cabot
Lodge, the friend
who had for us all,
through her infinite
charm and brilliant
intellectuality, a

fascination possessed by no other. She almost always sat at his table at the informal suppers, and, needless to say, those two were the centre of attraction. The table at which I myself sat that night had the distinguished presence of General Leonard Wood, General Young, and the French ambassador, Monsieur

Jusserand, one of my brother's favorite companions on the famous White House walks, hero of the true story of the time when on one of those same famous walks they inadvertently came to the river, into which my brother plunged, followed immediately by the dauntless French ambassador, who refused to "take off his gloves for fear of meeting the ladies"!

I spent one whole morning in the office during that visit, having asked my brother if I might sit quietly in a corner and listen to his interviews, to which request he gladly acceded. One after another, people filed in to see him. I made a few notes of the conversations. One of his first answers to some importunate person who wished him to take a stand on some special subject (at that time he was anxious not to embarrass his successor, Mr. Taft, by taking any special stands) was: "As Napoleon said to his marshals, 'I don't want to make pictures of myself.'"

In receiving Mr. Hall, the president of the Gridiron Club, he remarked that he (Theodore Roosevelt) had been one of the few people who used these dinners as "a field of missionary endeavor." Doctor Schick, of the Dutch Reformed Church, in which he had been a regular attendant, came to arrange for a good-by meeting at the church. To a man who came in to see him on the subject of industrial peace, he replied: "The President believes in conciliation in industrial problems." Endless subjects were brought up for his consideration, and many times I heard him say: "Remember, a new man is in the saddle, and there can't be two Presidents after March 4th." These notes were taken at the time, February, 1909, and are not the result of memory conveniently adjusted toward later happenings.

Every time I talked with my brother on the subject of the future, he repeated the fact that he was glad to plunge into the wilderness, so that no one could possibly think that he wanted a "finger in the pie" of the new administration. Over and over again he would say: "If I am where they can't get at me, and where I cannot hear what is going on, I cannot be supposed to wish to interfere with the methods of my successor."

One quiet evening when we had had a specially lovely family dinner, I turned to him and said: "Theodore, I want to give you a real present before you go away. What do you think you would like?" His eyes sparkled like a child who was about to

receive a specially
nice toy, and he said:
"Do you really want
to make me a real
present, Pussie? I
think I should like
a pigskin library."
"A pigskin library,"
I said, in great
astonishment. "What
is a pigskin library?"
He laughed, and said:
"Of course, I must
take a good many
books; I couldn't go
anywhere, not even

into jungles in Africa without a good many books. But also, of course, they are not very likely to last in ordinary bindings, and so I want to have them all bound in pigskin, and I would rather have that present than any other." The next day he dictated a list of the books which he wished, and the following evening added in his own handwriting a few more. The list is as follows:

BOOKS IN THE PIGSKIN LIBRARY

—Bible.
—Apocrypha.
—Borrow: Bible in Spain, Zingali, Lavengro, Wild Wales, The Romany Rye.
—Shakespeare.
—Spenser: Faerie

Queene.
—Marlowe.
—Mahan: Sea Power.
—Macaulay: History, Essays, Poems.
—Homer: Iliad, Odyssey.
—La Chanson de Roland.
—Nibelungenlied.
—Carlyle: Frederick the Great.
—Shelley: Poems.
—Bacon: Essays.
—Lowell: Literary Essays, Biglow

Papers.
-Emerson: Poems.
-Longfellow.
-Tennyson.
-Poe: Tales, Poems.
-Keats.
-Milton: Paradise Lost (Books I and II).
-Dante: Inferno (Carlyle's translation).
-Holmes: Autocrat, Over the Teacups.
-Bret Harte: Poems, Tales of the Argonauts, Luck of

Roaring Camp.
–Browning:Selections.
–Crothers: Gentle Reader, Pardoner's Wallet.
–Mark Twain: Huckleberry Finn, Tom Sawyer.
–The Federalist.
–Bunyan's Pilgrim's Progress.
–Froissart.
–Gregorovius: Rome.
–Percy's Reliques.
–Euripides (Murray's translation): Bacchæ.

Hippolytus.
–Scott: Legend of Montrose, Antiquary. Guy Mannering, Rob Roy, Waverley.
–Cooper: Two Admirals, Pilot.
–Dickens: Pickwick, Mutual Friend.
–Thackeray: Vanity Fair, Pendennis.

The famous pigskin library, carried on the back of "burros," followed him into the jungles of Africa, and was his constant companion at the end of long days during which he had slain the mighty beasts of the tangled forests.

Immediately after that happy week at the White House, I was stricken by a great sorrow, the death of my youngest son by an accident. My brother came

to me at once, and
sustained me as no
one else could have
done, and his one
idea during those
next weeks was to
make me realize his
constant thought
and love, even in
the midst of those
thrilling last days
at the White House,
when among other
events he welcomed
home the great fleet
which had completed

its circle of the world.

A few days before the death of my boy, and immediately after that enchanting last visit to the house we had learned to regard as Theodore's natural home, he wrote me the last letter I received from him dated from the White House. It was written February 19, 1909:

"Darling Corinne:
Just a line to tell you
what I have already
told you, of how we
shall always think of
you and thank you
when we draw on
the 'Pigskin Library'
in Africa. It was
too dear of you to
give it to me. That
last night was the
pleasantest function
we had ever held
at the White House,
and I am so glad

that you and Douglas were there. Tell Douglas he cannot imagine how I have enjoyed the rides with him." The above was typewritten, but inserted in his own handwriting at the end of the note were the characteristic lines: "You blessèd person. I have revelled in having you down here. T. R."

ABOUT THE AUTHOR

Corinne Roosevelt Robinson was born in 1861. In 1911, she published her first poem, "The Call of Brotherhood", after encouragement by Edith Wharton. Active in politics, she was the first woman to second the nomination of a national party convention candidate;

speaking before a crowd of 14,000 in 1920.

ABOUT THE COVER

The photo on the cover is of President Theodore Roosevelt with his family. On his left is his young son Quentin, who became a pursuit pilot in World War I and died in aerial combat over France on Bastille Day, 1918.

WHAT WE'RE ABOUT

I started making Super Large Print books for my grandma. I wanted books that she could keep reading as her glaucoma and macular degeneration advanced. So I chose a font originally designed for people with dyslexia, because the letters are bold and easy to distinguish. It is set at 30 pt, nearly twice the size of traditional Large Print books.

Digital reading was too frustrating for my grandma. It could never offer the pleasures she had always associated with reading: the peacefulness of turning a page, the satisfaction in knowing a story has "this much left," and the comforting memories of adventure, companionship, and revelation she felt when seeing the cover of her favorite book. Part of what makes reading so relaxing and grounding is the tactile experience. I hope these books can bring joy to those who want to keep reading and to those who've never had the pleasure of curling up with a page turner.

Please let me know if these books are helpful to you and if you have any requests for new titles. To leave feedback and to see the complete and constantly updating catalog, please visit:

superlargeprint.com

MORE BOOKS AT:

superlargeprint.com

KEEP ON READING!

OBLIGATORY TINY PRINT: This story is in the public domain and published here under fair use laws. The Super Large Print logo is copyright of Super Large Print. The cover design may not be reproduced for commercial purposes. If you have questions or believe we've made a mistake, please let us know at superlargeprint@gmail.com. And thank you for helping this book find its way to a person who might appreciate it.

This book is set in a font designed by Abelardo Gonzalez called OpenDyslexic

ISBN 9781081588007